Christmas on the Prairie

by Joan Anderson
photographed by George Ancona

CLARION BOOKS · TICKNOR & FIELDS · NEW YORK

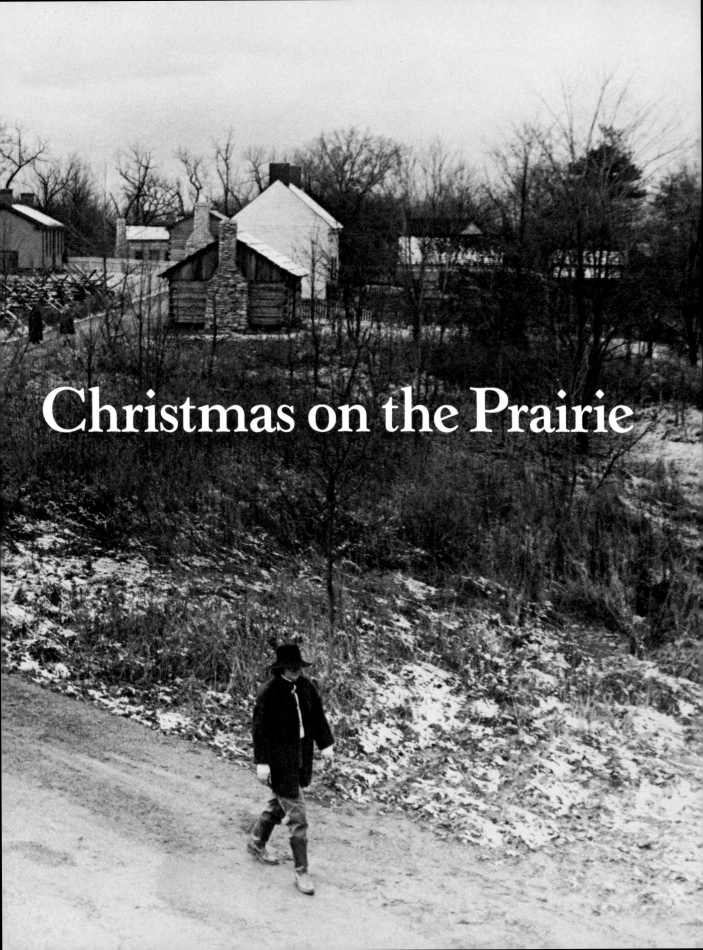

Christmas on the Prairie

To my mother, who taught me the true magic
and meaning of Christmas

J.A.

To Adolfo Leirner—*Boas Festas!*

G.A.

Clarion Books
Ticknor & Fields, a Houghton Mifflin Company
Text copyright © 1985 by Joan Anderson
Photographs copyright © 1985 by George Ancona

Printed in the U.S.A.

Library of Congress Cataloging in Publication Data
Anderson, Joan.
     Christmas on the prairie.

     Summary: Re-creates Christmas Eve and Christmas
morning in 1836 in the fictional village of Prairietown,
Indiana, to show how the holiday was celebrated in a
typical frontier community.
     1. Christmas—Indiana—Juvenile literature.
[1. Christmas—Indiana. 2. West (U.S.)—Social life and
customs] I. Ancona, George, ill. II. Title.
GT4986. I6A53 1985   394.2'68282'09772   85-4095
ISBN 0-89919-307-2

H 10 9 8 7 6 5 4 3 2 1

They have come hither from four corners of the globe, with manners and habits as different as nations from which they've sprung. Everything is new, just coming into existence, even Christmas.

Ray Allen Billington
American Frontier Heritage

Years ago in America, Christmas customs were much simpler than they are today. There were no greeting cards, no Christmas trees, and few store-bought gifts. In fact, some of the immigrant groups who came to America didn't believe Christmas should be celebrated at all.

Christmas on the Prairie re-creates Christmas Eve and Christmas morning in Prairietown, Indiana, in 1836. Ben Curtis, the local blacksmith, had moved his family to this frontier village from Canandaigua, a thriving town in New York State. Back home, the Curtis family had celebrated Christmas by blending their English customs with the old Dutch tradition of St. Nicholas.

"LAND SAKES, THOMAS, eat up. You too, Peter," Mother Curtis exclaimed while she dished out the scrambled eggs. "Why, this is a special day, don't you know? You two needn't be looking so glum."

Peter thought to himself as he finished his breakfast that Mother was always trying to make folks happy. But he didn't see how she could do much about Christmas Eve this year. The family's old friends were not around, and Mother couldn't get any fancies from New York City.

"Peter and Thomas," Father ordered, "you just have time to build the fire in the smithy before school. Hurry on over to the barn with me. Reuben and I have a full day of orders awaiting us." Reuben Pruitt, Father's apprentice, lived with the Curtises.

As the cold prairie wind nipped at their cheeks, Thomas said quietly to Peter, "It's Christmas Eve, and we have chores *and* school same as always. No one in Prairietown stops working for anything, not even Christmas."

"I know," Peter answered. "And I bet dumb old Schoolmaster Fergeson is making us go today just so he don't lose a day's pay. He has no idea what Christmas means."

After finishing their chores, the two boys scampered back to the house to walk Jenny and Edward to school. Mary Curtis hurried her children off, calling: "You come straight home, you hear? Aunt Ruth and I will have dough ready for speculaas."

At school the Curtis children settled down on hard, cold benches. The fireplace was never lit until just before lessons. That way the cold kept everyone alert. Both Peter and Thomas were thinking that school is the last place to be on Christmas Eve. The Schoolmaster talked about Christmas having been started by ancient people who worshipped the sun. Thomas felt for sure Master Fergeson knew nothing of what Christmas really meant, especially to the Curtis family.

"Let's get comfortable," Thomas whispered to Peter, rolling his eyes in boredom. "That way our noon meal will come faster."

During the noon break Thomas had an idea. "We could bar the Master," he whispered to the others.

"What's that?" a farm boy from down the road asked.

"It's a game," Thomas replied, enjoying the interest for his scheme. "We sneak inside the school when the Master's not looking, bolt the door, and when he tries to get in, we slip him a note."

"What does it say?" someone asked.

" 'No school for Christmas,' of course," Thomas replied with a grin.

Everyone agreed it was a good idea, so they darted inside and bolted the door.

"Let me in," Master Fergeson shouted, pounding on the door.

"Not today," the children shouted back.

"This is fun," Jenny Curtis giggled. But to their surprise, the knocking stopped.

"Let's wait a few minutes," Peter Curtis instructed. "If there's no sign of him, we'll make a run for it."

They waited and waited. The room was filling up with smoke. All began to cough.

So Peter unbolted the door, and they ran off in every direction. Thomas glanced back as he hopped the fence, wondering if the schoolhouse were burning down. Instead he saw the Master on the roof!

Old Fergeson had covered the chimney and smoked them out. Thomas was doubly glad their game had worked. He wished he had time to run back and grab the ladder.

The children of Prairietown were free and happy as they scattered about the village. They suddenly noticed another big treat. It was snowing!

A short time later, Peter left his sister and brothers peeking into the general store. Inside, they saw Mary Curtis and Mrs. McClure passing news.

"You best not sneak around Mother the day before Christmas," Peter called out as he ran off. He was already late for work in Father's shop.

Mr. Whitaker, the storekeeper, kept the potbelly stove going day and night. The store always had something new to sell that came by flatboat up the Ohio River and then by wagon from Indianapolis.

"Well," Mary Curtis asked, "what will you be doing for Christmas, Mrs. McClure?"

"We're expecting our boys home," Hannah McClure answered. "Of course, we aren't belonging to no religion and probably won't even read from the good book. We'll have a big dinner same as always."

"Well, I need a toy or two for my young'ns," Mary Curtis said, " 'specially for Thomas. The prairie isn't much for the kind of Christmas he had back east. He doesn't think St. Nicholas will find his way here."

Mr. Whitaker looked up from his account books. "I heard folks talking about gift-giving — even saw advertisements in *The Journal* suggesting such a thing. Next year I must order more fancies," he said, realizing that Christmas could prove profitable.

"Well, that would be a help," Mary Curtis said, "but, for now, I need four oranges."

"If there are any left," Hannah McClure said, in a gossipy way. "Mrs. Campbell pretty near bought out everything for her party."

"Oh, dear," Mary said, "no oranges?"

"Now don't fret," said Mr. Whitaker. "If what I have don't please you, there will be more today coming by wagon."

"Whatever is so important about oranges?" Hannah inquired.

"Oh, it's just a Dutch legend we took to back east. Supposedly there was a bishop named St. Nicholas who had a hankerin' for giving to the poor. One winter night he heard tell of three maidens who could not marry because they had no dowry. St. Nicholas, feeling they were deserving, dropped three bags of gold down their chimney. They awoke to magic and joy. I reckon, ever since, oranges have come to be sort of like gold— out here, anyway, what with the price being ten cents apiece!"

"There certainly are many strange customs connected to Christmas," Hannah McClure said. "I never thought this day would amount to anything." She shook her head and left the store.

Outside, the snow had stopped, but the sky remained gray and threatening. The merchandise cart had pulled up to the store.

It was loaded with goods and people too. Most were visitors come for the holiday, so the normally quiet street was abustle with activity. Still puzzling over Mary Curtis's Christmas ideas, Hannah hurried along, fighting against the strong prairie wind. In the distance, she saw her two sons and rushed to greet them.

Mary Curtis reached home before the children. Aunt Ruth had the kitchen table all set to roll and cut cookies. When the children arrived, the two women looked at their snow-covered clothing. "My goodness," Mother exclaimed, "you sure don't look like you've spent the whole day at lessons."

Edward and Jenny turned to Thomas but no one said a word.

"Gather round now and get to work," Mother continued. "If we hurry, we'll have time to take our cookies to the neighbors."

"Why don't we have all the fancy shapes we used to?" Thomas asked.

"Now you know right well we couldn't bring everything in the wagon when Father brought us here. Many things had to be left behind. These cookies might not look as pretty, but they'll taste just as good."

The kitchen did have a smell of Christmas, Thomas had to admit. But Mother had a faraway look in her eyes as she remembered Canandaigua.

"Maybe your father can cut us a special mold for next year. When I was little, your grandmother would mix together all sorts of spices and sugars to make the most special dough of all. When she was finished, out of the oven popped a giant two-foot cookie in the shape of St. Nicholas. She would then paint his robes red and his beard white with colored frosting. We could never quite believe that a cookie could be so real. And then there would be a party and everyone would eat him up!

"Yes, indeed," she said, while wiping the last cup dry. "Father will just have to make us a mold for such a cookie."

After the cookies were baked, Aunt Ruth filled a basket with them. Then Mother and the children were off visiting. They stopped at the barn, hoping Peter could come along. But even though Father had his good strong apprentice, Reuben, to help, Peter had to stay. "I have to resteel this ax for a man down in Noblesville before tonight," Father explained. "If we keep working now, we'll be ready to start celebrating by nightfall."

It was late afternoon as the Curtises walked along. Thomas was excited because visiting was so much a part of the Christmas he remembered. He was also secretly glad that he wasn't old enough to be his father's helper, like Peter.

"We'll stop at Widow Bucher's house first," Mother announced. "It's important to pay a call on those who are alone at Christmas. If the snow starts up again, her children might not be making it home."

The Widow was so excited to see the Curtises that she ushered them right into her little cabin.

"We brought you some special cookies," Mother said, placing them on the table.

"Well, thank you," the Widow exclaimed, pleased by the thoughtful gesture. She looked at Edward and Jenny. "It don't seem long since my young'ns were your age. My late husband Jacob used to play Belznickel on Christmas Eve. Have you ever heard of Belz?"

"No," Jenny said, her eyes all round and curious.

"Well," the Widow began, "he was an old man, dressed in odd clothes, who came banging at the door. My young'ns were always frightened so they hid behind my skirts. Once inside, Belznickel would ask: 'Have the children been good this year?'

"Before I could answer, he would pull out a big stick in order to spank them," the Widow continued. "I would quickly answer yes and he would promptly drop the stick, reach into his pockets, and throw love cookies and nuts about. As the young'ns scampered to collect the goodies, Belz would disappear."

"Now what my Sarah and Hiram didn't know was that my husband Jacob was playing Belznickel. Jacob would change his clothes and return to the house. The children always said, 'Oh, Pa, you missed Belznickel again.' And he would answer, 'You don't say? Come sit upon my lap and tell me about his visit.' He'd play some old Lutheran hymns on his fiddle and we'd always read from the Book of St. Luke."

The Widow had tears in her eyes. Mary Curtis swallowed quickly and nudged the children toward the door.

"We must be getting along, Widow Bucher," she said. "Good Christmas to you."

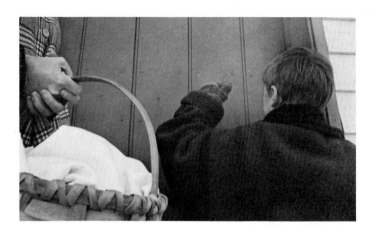

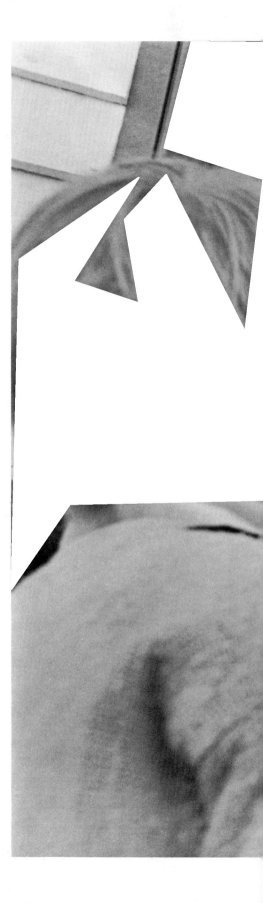

They stopped next at the Fentons'. Mary Curtis had heard that Mr. Fenton was laid up with a sickness, so they knocked ever so gently. They didn't expect to be greeted by a loud voice that didn't sound sick at all.

"Who's there?"

"It's the Curtis family come to wish you a good Christmas," Mother answered.

"Christmas! Christmas!" Mr. Fenton shouted, as he swung open his door. "Don't you know Christmas is a heathen belief? It don't say nothing in the Bible about celebrating Christmas. You just go home and read Jeremiah about stayin' away from pagan practices. Folks use Christmas as an excuse for hollerin' and carryin' on. We don't hold to that in this house." He slammed the door.

"Why was he so angry?" Thomas asked.

"I reckon some folks such as the Fentons do only as the Bible says," Mother sighed.

Just then they heard a shotgun blast. Rowdies were riding into town, singing and carrying on. They didn't look like they meant any harm, but Mary Curtis rushed the children toward the Campbell house anyway.

"Them boys have been gettin' into the squeezin's," she said. "No telling what they might do."

"Well, old Mr. Fenton did say folks were following after their own desires," said Thomas. He never remembered such carrying on back east. Life on the prairie was full of surprises, he thought.

They spotted Doctor Campbell with his horse all draped in cedar sprigs.

"Good Christmas, y'all," Doc Campbell called out in his Kentucky drawl. "The Missus needed a few more greens to decorate for the party. She's trying to make everything look like our home back in Lexington. Will you and the Mister be joining us tonight?" he inquired.

"Oh, no," Mother answered, wistfully. "Mr. Curtis says Christmas Eve is a time just for family."

"Then you must stop in and sample the treats," he insisted.

Mrs. Campbell greeted Mary Curtis and the children. Thomas couldn't believe all the fancy food. The house was decorated with greens and red satin ribbons. Everything reminded Thomas of Canandaigua. He wished for Mother's sake that she could go to the party, just for a little while.

"There's enough Christmas here to fill up all of Prairietown," he whispered to Mother. She smiled back.

It was hard to leave such a pretty place. But it was almost dark, so the Curtises wished Mrs. Campbell Good Christmas and hurried towards their own house.

Back home Thomas gathered extra wood for a cozy Christmas Eve fire. It had been a busy day, just like the day before Christmas always had been back east. Aunt Ruth had supper prepared. Peter, Reuben, and Father were waiting, having closed up the shop in plenty of time to celebrate. It would remain closed all the next day, just like Father always did on Christmas.

They sat down to supper. Father said the blessing. Suddenly Thomas felt Christmas surrounding him. There was snow on the ground for St. Nicholas, company was visiting all over Prairietown, and Mother and Father were trying to keep everything the same as always.

After supper, Aunt Ruth and Reuben went off to the Campbell party. Thomas could imagine all the merrymaking—singing, laughing, and eating that delicious food. He could hear the distant sounds of carols as some folks made their way up Old River Road. It sounded like Christmas in Canandaigua, even felt that way, only this was happening in Prairietown!

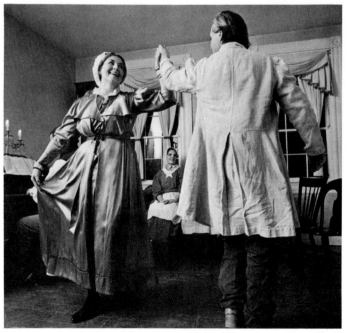

Soon Mother called to the children, "Gather 'round. Father is sitting by the fire ready to read his poem." She set out mugs of hot chocolate and a bowl of popcorn.

So Peter, Thomas, Edward, and Jenny got comfortable around the fire, which seemed to be burning especially bright.

"Now, children, listen carefully," Ben Curtis said. "Your grandfather used to read me this poem when I was a young'n."

As Father read, Thomas grew more and more excited about St. Nicholas and his gifts for good boys and girls. As soon as the poem was finished, they rushed to hang their stockings on the mantelpiece. Thomas wished hard for a pocketknife. Everything seemed the same as always—the poem, the hot chocolate, the stockings. But wait a minute. Something was missing.

Where were the wooden shoes? If Mother had left them behind, St. Nicholas might never come. As Thomas's mind raced in panicky thoughts, Mother appeared with Father's big old wooden shoes.

Peter raced to the barn for a handful of hay for St. Nicholas's horse, while Jenny went to the kitchen for carrots. Maybe Thomas would get his pocketknife after all.

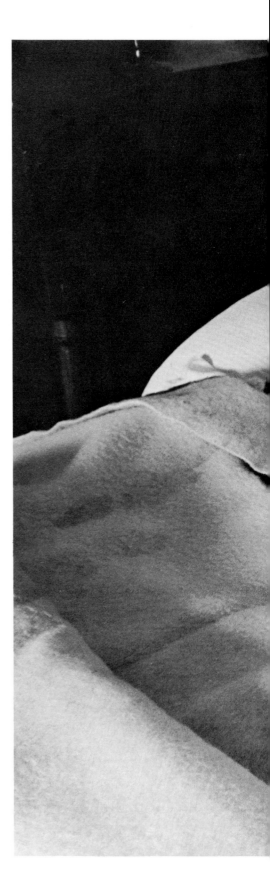

Finally, it was time for bed. The boys snuggled together to keep warm as the cold prairie wind howled outside.

The last thing Thomas heard before he fell off to sleep was the sound of Father's fiddle. On special nights he would get it out and play for Mother. The squeaky strains of "Joy to the World" filled the house, and Mother began to sing in her sweet, soft voice:

Joy to the world!
The Lord is come.
Let earth receive her King;
Let ev'ry heart, prepare him room,
and heav'n and nature sing...

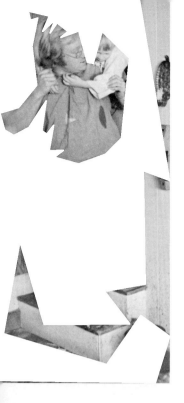

Early the next morning, Father called up to the children, "Good Christmas, Good Christmas, everyone. St. Nicholas sure did a fine job of getting on out to Prairietown!"

The Curtis children jumped out of bed, scrambled headlong down the tiny staircase, and bounded into the front chamber. They stopped in their tracks to stare at the fireplace. There upon the mantelpiece were beautiful golden oranges and stockings full of goodies. On the floor below, the wooden shoes were empty of hay and carrots, so Thomas knew St. Nicholas's horse had had a good meal. But now the shoes were filled with tiny wrapped surprises. That had never happened in Canandaigua.

Peter handed Thomas his stocking. Sticking right out of the top was the grandest pocketknife he had ever seen. Jenny found a doll in her stocking, and Edward got a curious marble game. Peter received a book he had wished for ever since the family left the East. In addition, each stocking held lemon drops, rock candy, and marzipan animals.

"Christmas comes everywhere, even on the prairie," Thomas said in wonder.

"Yes," Mother replied, with a gentle smile. "Wherever people are, they can make it happen."

Our Thanks

To the staff and interpreters at the living history museum of Conner Prairie Pioneer Settlement near Noblesville, Indiana, where this book was photographed. Prairietown, the name given to the village at Conner Prairie, is a fictional community. It is based on historical records of typical settlements in Indiana in the early 1800s. The people of Prairietown reflect the different ethnic and religious backgrounds of the pioneers in the West at that time.

We are especially grateful to Becky Marciniak, LuAnn Howard, and Susan Cain, who coordinated all the photographic sessions; and to Steven Stearns and David Vanderstel, who patiently answered every conceivable historical question. We are most grateful to Thomas Sanders and his three beautiful children, who portrayed Thomas, Jenny, and Edward Curtis; to P.J., who played Peter Curtis; and to June Hamblen, who was perfect as Mary Curtis, their pioneer mother.

In the New York area, we are grateful to Philipsburg Manor in North Tarrytown, New York, where the St. Nicholas cookie and other still-life photos were taken; to Robin Wilkins, for his cameo appearance as Belznickel; and to Gay McIndoe, for the use of her antique toy collection.

Good Christmas to all!

Joan Anderson & George Ancona